D1254455

Jill Foran

Weigl

Published by Weigl Educational Publishers Limited
6325 10 Street S.E.
Calgary, Alberta
T2H 2Z9

Website: www.weigl.com
Copyright ©2010 Weigl Educational Publishers Limited
All rights reserved. No part of this publication may be reproduced, stored in a retrieval system, or transmitted in any
form or by any means, electronic, mechanical, photocopying, recording, or otherwise, without the prior written permission
of the publisher.

Library and Archives Canada Cataloguing in Publication data available upon request.
Fax 403-233-7769 for the attention of the Publishing Records department.

ISBN 978-1-55388-519-1 (hard cover)
ISBN 978-1-55388-524-5 (soft cover)

Printed in the United States of America
1 2 3 4 5 6 7 8 9 0 13 12 11 10 09

Editor: Heather C. Hudak
Design: Terry Paulhus

Every reasonable effort has been made to trace ownership and to obtain permission to reprint copyright material. The
publishers would be pleased to have any errors or omissions brought to their attention so that they may be corrected
in subsequent printings.

Weigl acknowledges Getty Images as its primary image supplier for this title.

We gratefully acknowledge the financial support of the Government of Canada through the Book Publishing Industry
Development Program (BPIDP) for our publishing activities.

Contents

What is Victoria Day?........................ 4

Birthday Celebration 6

British Heritage.............................. 8

A National Holiday 10

The End of Winter 12

Parades and Parties........................14

A Special Song 16

Bread and Cheese Day 18

Celebrating a Soldier 20

Queen Elizabeth II 22

Glossary/Index............................... 24

What is Victoria Day?

Each year on the Monday before May 25, Canadians honour Queen Victoria's birthday. This holiday is known as Victoria Day. Queen Victoria was born on May 24, 1819. She became queen of **Great Britain** when she was 18 years old.

4

Birthday Celebration

Queen Victoria ruled the British Empire from 1837 to 1901. This is longer than any other person. At the time, Canada was part of Queen Victoria's kingdom. The people of present-day Ontario began celebrating Queen Victoria's birthday in 1845.

6

British Heritage

In 1867, Canada became a country and was no longer under British rule. Canadians across the country continued to celebrate this special day. Victoria Day pays tribute to Queen Victoria's great work throughout her kingdom and Canada's British **heritage**.

8

A National Holiday

For many years, Victoria Day was celebrated on the queen's birthday. It took place on May 25 if May 24 fell on a Sunday. This was so that special events did not disrupt church services. In 1952, the Government of Canada stated that Victoria Day would always take place on the Monday before May 25.

The End of Winter

Victoria Day is a symbol of the end of winter. Many people do not have to work or go to school on Victoria Day. They can take part in many fun events, such as hiking and camping.

Parades and Parties

Some people have picnics or large parties on Victoria Day. Others play in sporting events. Many cities and towns have fireworks displays. Victoria, British Columbia, was named after Queen Victoria. On Victoria Day, this city has a parade with bands, floats, and clowns. More than 120,000 people watch the parade on TV and in person each year.

A Special Song

God Save the Queen is Canada's royal **anthem**. This special song is played at many Victoria Day events.

God Save The Queen

God save our gracious Queen,
Long live our noble Queen,
God save the Queen:
Send her victorious,
Happy and glorious,
Long to reign over us:
God save the Queen.
O Lord, our God, arise,
Scatter her enemies,
And make them fall.
Confound their politics,
Frustrate their knavish tricks,
On Thee our hopes we fix,
God save us all.
Thy choicest gifts in store,
On her be pleased to pour;
Long may she reign:
May she defend our laws,
And ever give us cause
To sing with heart and voice
God save the Queen.

Bread and Cheese Day

On the Victoria Day weekend, the Six Nations Reserve near Brantford, Ontario, celebrates Bread and Cheese Day. This tradition started in 1837. Queen Victoria thanked Aboriginal Peoples for helping Great Britain in many battles. She gave them bread and cheese as a gift.

Celebrating a Soldier

Canadians in Quebec celebrate Fête de Dollard des Ormeaux on the May long weekend. This holiday honours a **soldier** who fought for New France in the 1600s. New France was the land the French owned in North America until 1763. French Canadians pay tribute to their heritage on this day.

Queen Elizabeth II

Victoria Day also honours the birth of Queen Elizabeth II. She is the current queen and one of the longest rulers of Great Britain. Her real birthday is April 21.

Glossary

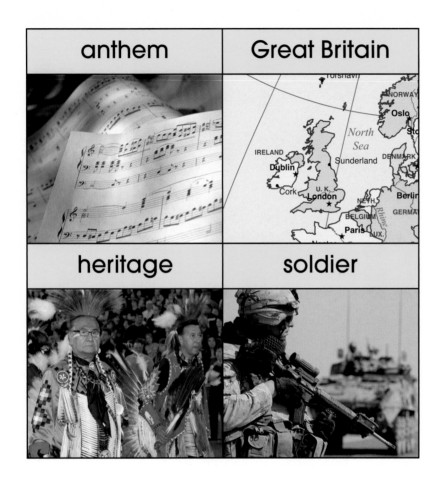

anthem	Great Britain
heritage	soldier

Index

Fête de Dollard des Ormeaux 20

Great Britain 4, 18, 22

May 25 4, 10

Quebec 20
Queen Elizabeth II 22

Six Nations Reserve 18